The Golden Gate Bridge

by Kevin Blake

Consultant:
Mary Currie, Retired Public Affairs Director
Golden Gate Bridge, Highway and Transportation District
San Francisco, California

BEARPORT
PUBLISHING
New York, New York

Credits

Cover and Title Page, © Travel Stock/Shutterstock; 2–3, © Irina Kosareva/Shutterstock; 4L, San Francisco History Center, San Francisco Public Library; 4R, © Andrew Zarivny/ Shutterstock; 5, San Francisco History Center, San Francisco Public Library; 6L, © Mapping Specialists, Ltd.; 6R, © Universal Images Group North America LLC (Lake County Discovery Museum)/Alamy; 7, © ClassicStock/Alamy; 8–9, Library of Congress; 9T, © Vereschchagin Dmitry/Shutterstock; 10L, San Francisco History Center, San Francisco Public Library; 10–11, San Francisco History Center, San Francisco Public Library; 12, © stocker1970/ Shutterstock; 13L, © Alessandro Colle/Shutterstock; 13R, © holbox/Shutterstock; 14, San Francisco History Center, San Francisco Public Library; 15, © Everett Historical/ Shutterstock; 16L, San Francisco History Center, San Francisco Public Library; 16R, San Francisco History Center, San Francisco Public Library; 17, San Francisco History Center, San Francisco Public Library; 18, From the holdings of the Golden Gate Bridge, Highway and Transportation District; 19T, San Francisco History Center, San Francisco Public Library; 19B, © AP Photo; 20, San Francisco History Center, San Francisco Public Library; 21T, Joe Ross/tinyurl.com/zdr3dg3/CC BY-SA 2.0; 21B, San Francisco History Center, San Francisco Public Library; 22, © AP Photo; 23, © AP Photo; 24T, © Zuma Press Inc/Alamy; 24B, San Francisco History Center, San Francisco Public Library; 25T, Library of Congress; 25B, © Sueddeutsche Zeitung Photo/Alamy; 26, USGS/tinyurl.com/gnd853p/Public domain; 27, © Luciano Mortula/Shutterstock; 28–29, © Hugo Brizard - YouGoPhoto/ Shutterstock; © holbox/Shutterstock; 32, © Rich Niewiroski Jr./tinyurl.com/zfhg7xk/ CC BY 2.5.

Publisher: Kenn Goin
Senior Editor: Joyce Tavolacci
Creative Director: Spencer Brinker
Design: The Design Lab
Photo Researcher: Editorial Directions, Inc.

Library of Congress Cataloging-in-Publication Data

Names: Blake, Kevin, 1978– author.
Title: The Golden Gate Bridge / by Kevin Blake.
Description: New York, New York : Bearport Publishing, [2017] | Series:
  American places : from vision to reality | Audience: Ages 7 to 12. |
  Includes bibliographical references and index.
Identifiers: LCCN 2016018089 (print) | LCCN 2016021942 (ebook) | ISBN
  9781944102449 (library binding) | ISBN 9781944997113 (ebook)
Subjects: LCSH: Golden Gate Bridge (San Francisco, Calif.)—Juvenile
  literature. | Golden Gate Bridge (San Francisco,
  Calif.)—History—Juvenile literature. | Suspension
  bridges—California—San Francisco—Design and
  construction—History—Juvenile literature. | San Francisco
  (Calif.)—Buildings, structures, etc.—Juvenile literature.
Classification: LCC TG25.S225 B55 2017 (print) | LCC TG25.S225 (ebook) | DDC
  624.2/30979461—dc23

LC record available at https://lccn.loc.gov/2016018089

For more information, write to Bearport Publishing Company, Inc., 45 West 21st Street, Suite 3B, New York, New York 10010. Printed in the United States of America.

10 9 8 7 6 5 4 3 2 1

Contents

Disaster!

It was February 17, 1937, in Northern California. Hundreds of feet above the cold, swirling waters of San Francisco Bay, construction worker Slim Lambert was hard at work helping to build the Golden Gate Bridge. As Slim and his crew balanced on a narrow platform attached to the bridge, disaster struck. The platform broke and ripped through the safety net below. Twelve men, including Slim, **hurtled** 220 feet (67 m) through the air toward the **frigid** water.

Slim Lambert

In February, the average water temperature of San Francisco Bay is a chilly 50°F (12°C).

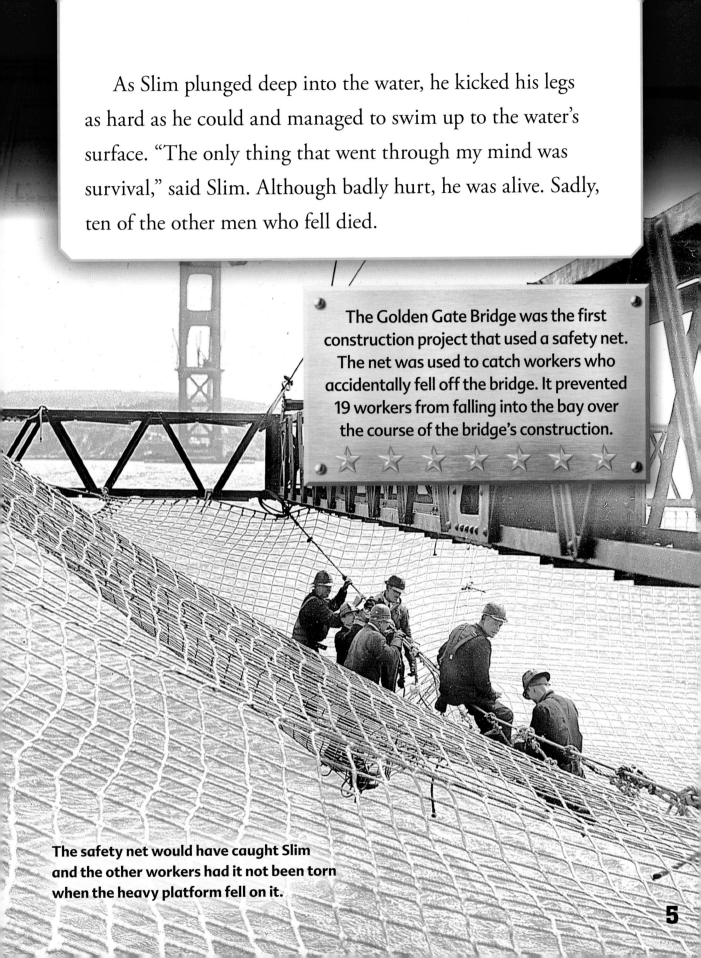

As Slim plunged deep into the water, he kicked his legs as hard as he could and managed to swim up to the water's surface. "The only thing that went through my mind was survival," said Slim. Although badly hurt, he was alive. Sadly, ten of the other men who fell died.

The Golden Gate Bridge was the first construction project that used a safety net. The net was used to catch workers who accidentally fell off the bridge. It prevented 19 workers from falling into the bay over the course of the bridge's construction.

The safety net would have caught Slim and the other workers had it not been torn when the heavy platform fell on it.

A Great Need

Despite the terrible **tragedy**, work on the Golden Gate Bridge continued at a fast pace. The people of San Francisco desperately needed the bridge. Why? San Francisco sits on a **peninsula** with water on three sides: the Pacific Ocean, San Francisco Bay, and a narrow passage of water called the Golden Gate **strait**. Before the bridge was built, the only way people could cross the strait and travel to and from nearby Marin County was by ferryboat.

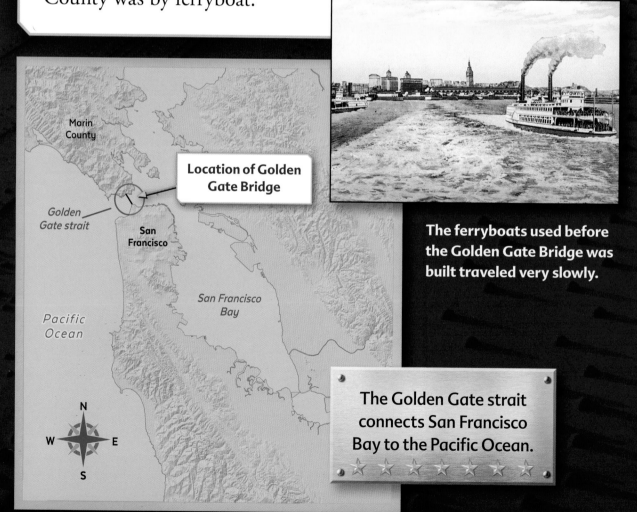

Location of Golden Gate Bridge

Marin County

Golden Gate strait

San Francisco

Pacific Ocean

San Francisco Bay

N W E S

The ferryboats used before the Golden Gate Bridge was built traveled very slowly.

The Golden Gate strait connects San Francisco Bay to the Pacific Ocean.

In the 1930s, the **population** of San Francisco was growing at a fast rate. During this time, as new roadways were being built in California and in other parts of America, many people were purchasing cars. A new bridge would mean more people could reach San Francisco by car. It would also be much faster to drive into and out of the city from the north.

An automobile in the 1930s

An Impossible Feat

Where did the idea for a bridge come from? Two businessmen first suggested a bridge that spanned the Golden Gate strait in the mid-1800s. However, there were a number of big challenges that prevented the idea from becoming a reality. For one thing, the bridge would need to be huge, **spanning** a strait that stretches more than a mile (1.6 km) wide. At the time, a bridge of that size had never been built before.

San Francisco in about 1900

The Golden Gate strait has big waves and strong **currents**, which churn up the water.

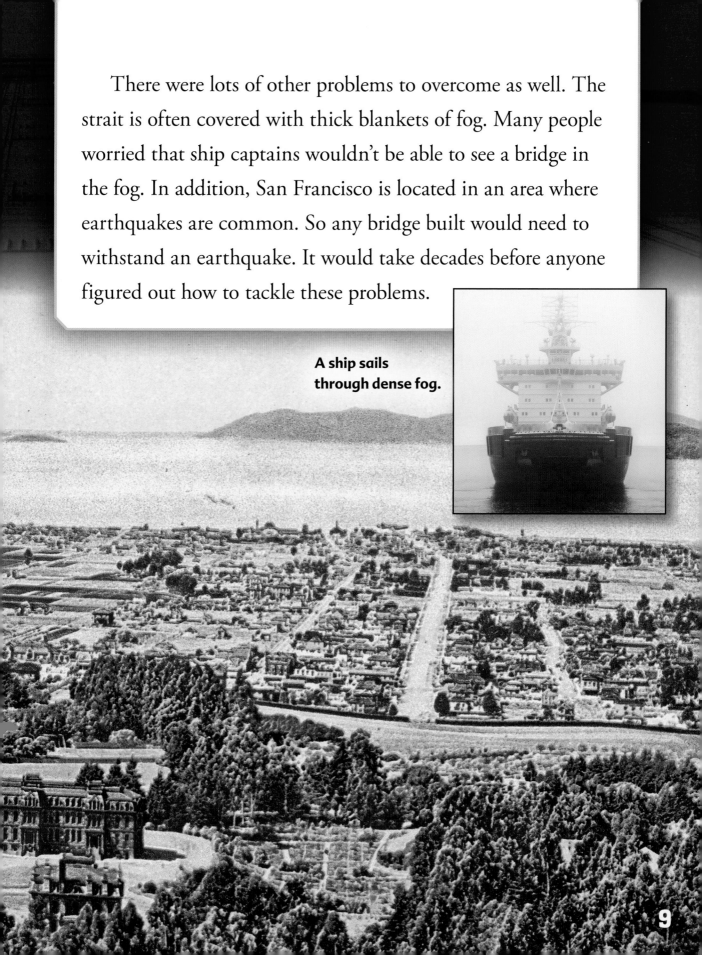

There were lots of other problems to overcome as well. The strait is often covered with thick blankets of fog. Many people worried that ship captains wouldn't be able to see a bridge in the fog. In addition, San Francisco is located in an area where earthquakes are common. So any bridge built would need to withstand an earthquake. It would take decades before anyone figured out how to tackle these problems.

A ship sails through dense fog.

9

The Dreamer

In 1916, the idea for a bridge was brought up again by a former **engineer** named James Wilkins. His enthusiasm got people, especially San Francisco City Engineer Michael O'Shaughnessy, very excited. Michael invited a few well-known engineers to submit plans for the bridge. One of the engineers was a young man from Ohio named Joseph Strauss. Joseph dreamed of building "the biggest thing of its kind that a man could build."

The engineer Joseph Strauss had designed more than 400 bridges.

Joseph's original design for the bridge

Michael liked Joseph's plan. Plus, Joseph claimed he could build the bridge for $27 million, almost half of what other engineers had proposed. However, when Joseph sent in his completed design for a cantilever bridge, the people of San Francisco thought it was ugly. One person said it looked "like an upside-down rattrap." Joseph immediately went back to the drawing board.

A cantilever bridge uses large **horizontal** beams that jut out sideways from either end of the bridge. The beams support the **deck**, or the part of the bridge where the roadway is located.

A Suspension Bridge

Working with a team of expert engineers, Joseph came up with an entirely new plan. This time he proposed a huge suspension bridge—the longest one of its kind that had ever been designed. Unlike a cantilever bridge, a suspension bridge uses two tall towers to support two large **cables** that run horizontally above the deck. The large cables then support many smaller **vertical** cables that hold the weight of the deck.

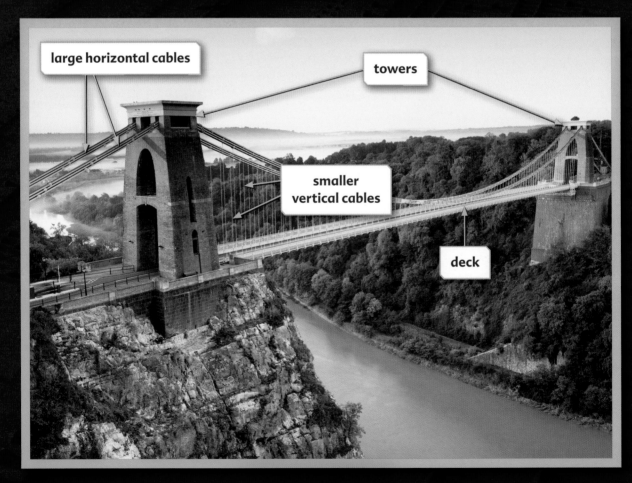

large horizontal cables

towers

smaller vertical cables

deck

A suspension bridge

With advice from other experts, including the architects Irving and Gertrude Morrow, the look of the bridge was also transformed. The new bridge's towers would be constructed in a bold style called **Art Deco**. The bridge would also be painted a rich, reddish-orange color that would help the structure stand out against the surrounding hills and water.

Art Deco was a popular style in the early 1900s. The Chrysler Building in New York City is one of the most famous Art Deco buildings in the world.

The United States Navy didn't like the color chosen for the bridge. They wanted the bridge to have black and yellow stripes to make it even more visible to passing ships in the heavy fog.

Brave Workers Wanted

With the design finally approved, construction of the Golden Gate Bridge began on January 5, 1933. Workers would have to deal with dense fog, strong winds, and freezing cold. They would also have to work at dizzying heights where the risk of falling would be a constant threat.

Joseph Strauss

Joseph Strauss reviews the final plans for the bridge with other experts.

Despite the dangers, thousands of men, including taxicab drivers, farmers, and a cowboy named Slim Lambert, lined up to work on the bridge. The project took place during the Great Depression—a time when people were **desperate** for work. Each worker could earn as much as $11 per day, which was good pay at the time. One supervisor remembered "there was always somebody waiting at the base of the tower for someone to fall off so they'd get a job."

Unemployed men wait on line for a free meal during the Great Depression.

The Great Depression lasted from 1929 to 1939. During that time, many people were out of work, had little food, or were homeless.

Two Piers

The first task for the workers was to build two large **piers** to support the two tall towers at either end of the bridge. Each pier would be an incredible 12 stories high. While the northern pier could be built on land, the southern pier had to be placed in the water. It wouldn't be an easy job. Tons of dirt and rock would need to be removed and concrete poured in its place.

The bridge workers were required to wear special equipment called hard hats to protect their heads.

Workers building one of the piers

As the concrete was poured, workers stirred it to remove any air bubbles, which could weaken the piers.

To build the southern pier, divers dove 100 feet (35 m) into the strait's cold, murky waters. Powerful currents and **choppy** water meant that even the strongest swimmers could work for only minutes at a time. The workers used special bombs to blast a giant hole in the ocean floor to create a spot for the base of the pier. The bombs were so powerful that when they exploded dozens of fish would fly out of the water and into the air! Concrete was then pumped into the hole to finish the pier.

Huge Towers

With the huge piers complete, the workers built the bridge's two graceful towers on top of them. Each tower would stretch 746 feet (227 m) into the sky—that's as tall as a skyscraper! To make the towers, workers would use more than 88,000 tons (79,832 metric tons) of **steel**.

The northern tower slowly takes shape.

From the outside, the towers each look like one solid piece of metal. However, workers made them out of hundreds of small empty **cells**, or cubes. Why? Placed together, the cubes helped strengthen the towers. To connect the cells, workers hammered more than one million extremely hot pieces of metal called **rivets** into the steel.

A worker connects the metal cells together with rivets.

The steel for the towers was made in Pennsylvania and then shipped through the **Panama Canal** to San Francisco Bay!

Workers raise the U.S. flag on the top of a finished tower.

19

The Main Cables

After the towers were finished, the workers installed the two main horizontal cables. Each cable measured 3 feet (0.9 m) across and weighed 12,000 tons (10,886 metric tons)! To make the cables as strong as possible, workers spun together tens of thousands of smaller metal strands—each about the width of a pencil. In total, more than 80,000 miles (128,748 km) of steel strands were woven together to create the cables.

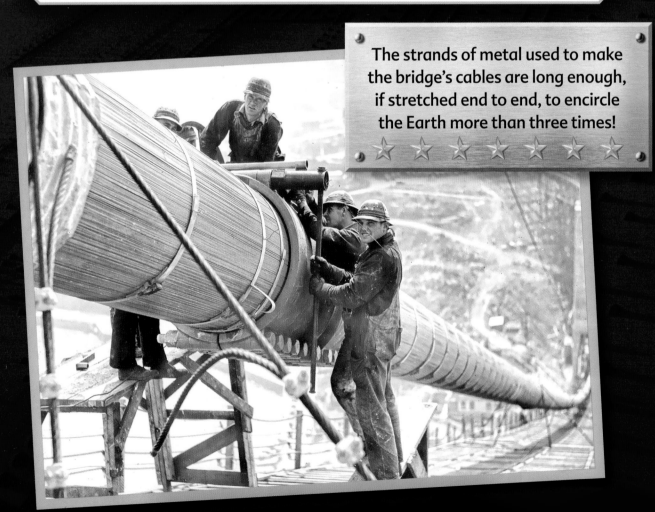

The strands of metal used to make the bridge's cables are long enough, if stretched end to end, to encircle the Earth more than three times!

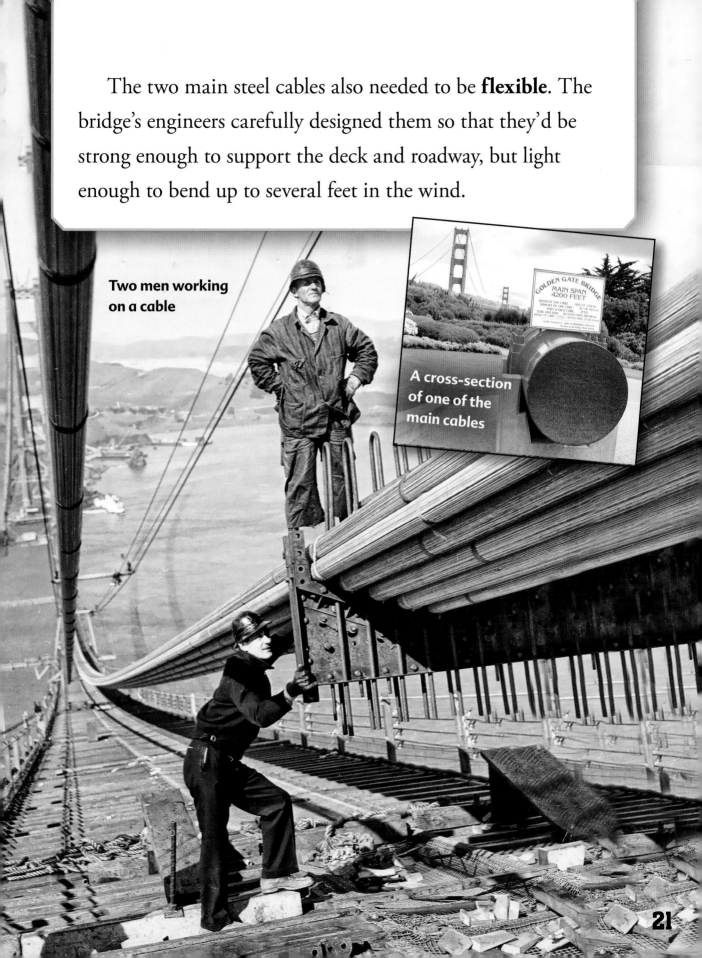

The two main steel cables also needed to be **flexible**. The bridge's engineers carefully designed them so that they'd be strong enough to support the deck and roadway, but light enough to bend up to several feet in the wind.

Two men working on a cable

A cross-section of one of the main cables

GOLDEN GATE BRIDGE
MAIN SPAN
4200 FEET

A Finished Bridge

From the main cables, the workers hung more than 250 pairs of smaller vertical cables called suspender ropes. These steel cables would hold up, or suspend, the roadway—similar to the way suspenders hold up pants! Finally, the workers installed steel **trusses** and long beams to support the deck and roadway. Then, as the last step, the steel deck was paved to make a road.

The steel trusses and the unfinished roadway

On April 19, 1937, construction was finally finished—about four years after the project started. In the end, 11 bridge workers lost their lives and the project had cost $35 million. However, it was considered one of the greatest engineering **feats** ever accomplished. Joseph Strauss was so pleased with the bridge that he wrote a poem called "The Mighty Task is Done."

When it was complete, the Golden Gate Bridge was the longest suspension bridge in the world. The *San Francisco Chronicle* called it a "thirty-five million dollar steel harp" because it looked like a giant stringed instrument.

Opening Day

San Francisco celebrated its new bridge with a two-day party. At 6:00 A.M. on May 27, 1937, the bridge opened to **pedestrians**. More than 18,000 lined up to cross the bridge. By the end of the day, more than 200,000 people had traveled across the Golden Gate Bridge.

People thought of interesting ways to cross the bridge on opening day—including on roller skates, stilts, and even on **unicycles**!

GOLDEN GATE BRIDGE FIESTA
San Francisco

OFFICIAL
PEDESTRIAN DAY
MAY 27, 1937
45150 Souvenir   25¢

Pedestrians purchased tickets to cross the bridge.

The next day was the official opening. President Franklin D. Roosevelt pressed a golden button back in the White House that signaled that the bridge was open for business! A hundred rockets soared into the sky and 500 aircraft zoomed by. The U.S. Navy sent 42 ships to celebrate the opening. That day, 32,000 vehicles passed over the bridge!

President Franklin Roosevelt

Cars crossing the bridge on May 28, 1937

The Big Test

By 1985, more than a billion cars had driven over the famous bridge. However, the Golden Gate had yet to face its biggest challenge. On October 17, 1989, a powerful earthquake hit the San Francisco Bay Area. Some roadways and buildings were badly damaged. The bridge, however, was unharmed. The bridge that many people said could never be built stood strong in even the most dangerous conditions.

A portion of a major highway in Oakland, California, crumbled from the force of the 1989 earthquake.

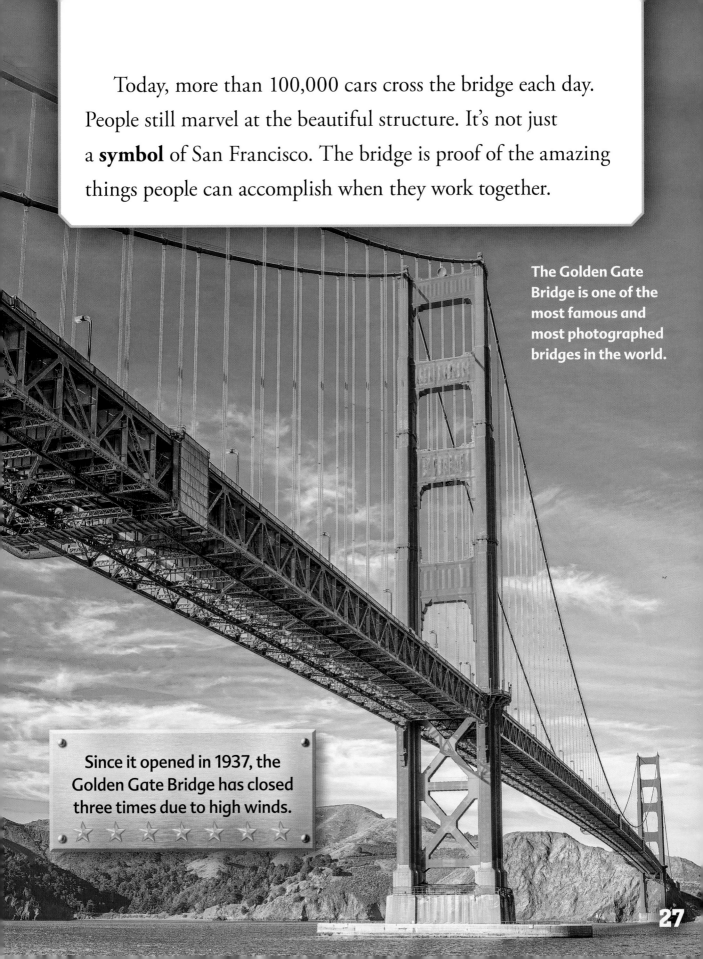

Today, more than 100,000 cars cross the bridge each day. People still marvel at the beautiful structure. It's not just a **symbol** of San Francisco. The bridge is proof of the amazing things people can accomplish when they work together.

The Golden Gate Bridge is one of the most famous and most photographed bridges in the world.

Since it opened in 1937, the Golden Gate Bridge has closed three times due to high winds.

The Golden Gate Bridge
BY THE NUMBERS

South Tower

Width of Bridge: 90 feet (27 m)

Total Weight of Bridge: 894,499 tons (811,476 metric tons)

Height of Towers Above the Deck: 500 feet (152 m)

Height of Towers Above the Water: 746 feet (227 m)

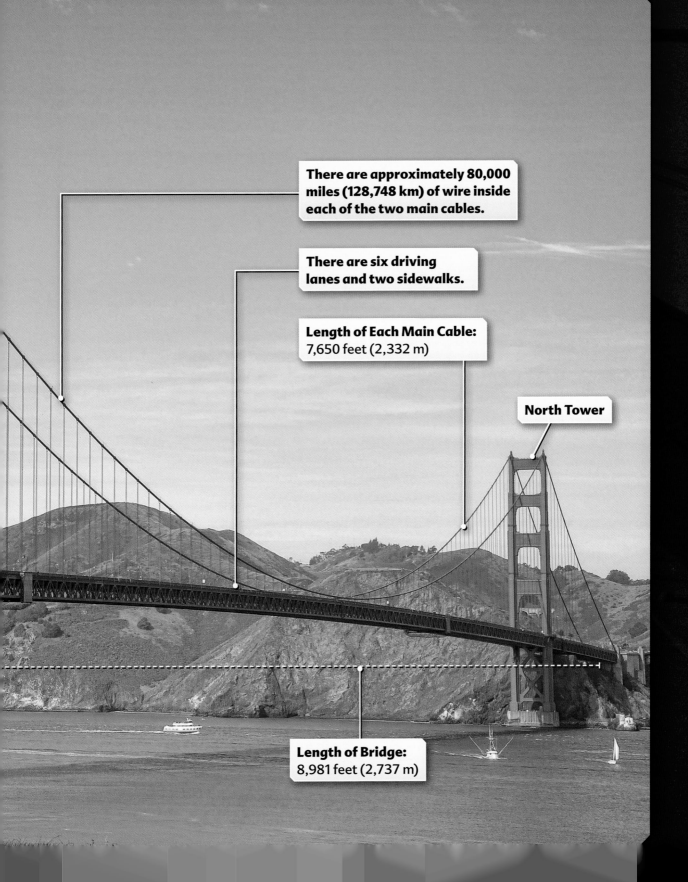

There are approximately 80,000 miles (128,748 km) of wire inside each of the two main cables.

There are six driving lanes and two sidewalks.

Length of Each Main Cable:
7,650 feet (2,332 m)

North Tower

Length of Bridge:
8,981 feet (2,737 m)

Glossary

Art Deco (ART DEK-oh) a style of art popular in the 1920s and 1930s that uses bold shapes and colors

cables (KAY-buhlz) thick ropes or wires

cells (SELZ) small cubes or boxes

choppy (CHOP-ee) rough

currents (KUR-uhnts) the movements of water in an ocean or river

deck (DEK) the platform on a bridge on which cars drive and people walk

desperate (DESS-pur-it) feeling hopeless; willing to do anything to change a situation

engineer (en-jun-NIHR) a person who designs and builds bridges, roads, buildings, or other structures

feats (FEETS) great deeds or accomplishments

flexible (FLEK-suh-buhl) able to bend

frigid (FRIJ-id) very cold

horizontal (hor-uh-ZON-tuhl) flat; level with the ground

hurtled (HUR-tuhld) moving at great speed

Panama Canal (PAN-uh-mah kuh-NAL) the human-made waterway that connects the Atlantic and Pacific Oceans

pedestrians (PUH-dess-tree-uhns) people walking

peninsula (puh-NIN-suh-luh) land that's surrounded by water on three sides

piers (PEERZ) pillars that support bridges

population (*pop*-yuh-LAY-shuhn) the total number of people living in a place

rivets (RIV-its) small pins used to hold two pieces of metal together

spanning (SPAN-ning) extending across

steel (STEEL) a hard metal often used in construction

strait (STRAYT) a narrow strip of water that connects two larger bodies of water

symbol (SIM-buhl) a design or an object that stands for something else

tragedy (TRAJ-uh-dee) a terrible event that causes great sadness or suffering

trusses (TRUS-iz) frames used to support or strengthen something else

unicycles (YOO-nuh-sye-kuhls) bicycle-like vehicles that have only one wheel and no handlebars

vertical (VUR-tuh-kuhl) upright, or in an up-and-down direction

Bibliography

American Experience, Golden Gate Bridge: www.pbs.org/wgbh/
americanexperience/films/goldengate/

MacDonald, Donald. *Golden Gate Bridge: History and Design of an Icon.* San
Francisco: Chronicle Books (2008).

Schwartz, Harvey. *Building the Golden Gate Bridge: A Workers' Oral History.*
Seattle, WA: University of Washington Press (2015).

Van Der Zee, John. *The Gate: The True Story of the Design and Construction
of the Golden Gate Bridge.* Backinprint.com (2000).

Read More

Hoena, Blake. *Building the Golden Gate Bridge (You Choose: Engineering
Marvels).* North Mankato, MN: Capstone (2014).

Stanborough, Rebecca. *Golden Gate Bridge (Engineering Marvels).* North
Mankato, MN: Capstone (2016).

Learn More Online

To learn more about the Golden Gate Bridge, visit:
www.bearportpublishing.com/AmericanPlaces

Index

About the Author

Kevin Blake lives in Providence, Rhode Island, with his wife, Melissa, and son, Sam. He's lucky to have driven over the Golden Gate Bridge!